POPE
JOHN PAUL II

PILGRIM OF PEACE

POPE
JOHN PAUL II

P I L G R I M   O F   P E A C E

Homilies and Addresses by
JOHN PAUL II

Foreword by
JOSEPH CARDINAL BERNARDIN
Archbishop of Chicago

Photographs by
ARTURO MARI
Official Vatican Photographer

H A R M O N Y   B O O K S   ·   N E W   Y O R K

Published by Harmony Books, a division of Crown Publishers, Inc.,
225 Park Avenue South, New York, New York 10003

HARMONY and colophon are trademarks of Crown Publishers, Inc.

Manufactured in Japan

Library of Congress Cataloging-in-Publication Data
John Paul II, Pope, 1920–   Pope John Paul II, pilgrim of peace.
1. John Paul II. Pope, 1920–   —Journeys. I. Mari, Arturo. II. Title.
BX1378.5.J584   1987   252'.02   86-14253
ISBN 0-517-56423-8

10 9 8 7 6 5 4 3 2 1

First Edition

A Hannibal Book
Text Selection by Dr. Alfred Bloch
Book design by Kathleen Westray and Ed Sturmer,
Design and Printing Productions

CONTENTS

FOREWORD

by Joseph Cardinal Bernardin,
Archbishop of Chicago

In the seven and a half years of his pontificate, Pope John Paul II has averaged more than four trips a year outside Italy. His "pilgrimages of peace" have already taken him to five continents, and he plans to visit a sixth in the near future.

The specific themes of his travels are directly related to the culture and needs of each country. Nevertheless, the basic premise of all these pastoral visitations gives them an underlying unity. His words spoken in Nicaragua in March 1983 could be applied to all of his pilgrimages. There he described himself as a "messenger of peace, sustainer of hope, servant of faith."

His peacemaking efforts are based on the gospel mandate of justice, compassion, human solidarity, and love. Although the theme of peace flows throughout his pontificate, he has spoken about it nowhere more passionately than at Hiroshima, at the very site of the 1945 nuclear explosion that ushered in the Atomic Age with its potential promise and destructive power.

The Pope's many addresses in the southern hemisphere, in the developing or "Third" world, show a keen awareness of the poverty and suffering of millions of his brothers and sisters. He is an eloquent advocate for the poor, challenging oppressive structures and governments, and sustaining the hope of the poor by showing clearly that he stands in solidarity with them.

In the northern hemisphere, in the developed nations of Europe and North America, with their long-standing Catholic tradition, he challenges the faithful to find their soul once again, to withstand the pressures of consumerism and materialism, and to give faithful witness to gospel values and Church teaching.

As a servant of faith the Holy Father constantly and consistently discusses the proper relationship between the gospel and culture. Because of the pluralistic context of many nations he visits, he reaches out to others in ecumenical and inter-faith gatherings. He frequently points out the necessity of unity within the human family so that justice may be established and peace may flourish.

Pope John Paul II has a special place in his heart—clearly reflected in his pilgrimages of peace—for the youth of the world. He recognizes in them the future of the human family and calls on them to remain faithful to the religious heritage that they have received and to take their rightful place in the Church and society in service of their brothers and sisters.

This beautifully illustrated book of carefully selected passages from the Holy Father's homilies and addresses throughout the world makes available his pastoral message and challenge to many readers. May this words inspire all of us to imitate his example and become "pilgrims of peace."

POPE
JOHN PAUL II

PILGRIM OF PEACE

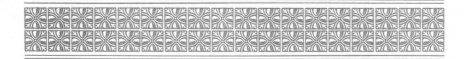

MEXICO

January 25 — February 1, 1979

Perhaps one of the most obvious weaknesses of present-day civilization lies in an inadequate view of man. Without doubt, our age is the one in which man has been most written and spoken of, the age of the forms of humanism and the age of anthropocentrism. Nevertheless it is paradoxically also the age of man's deepest anxiety about his identity and his destiny, the age of man's abasement to previously unsuspected levels, the age of human values trampled on as never before.

How is this paradox explained? We can say that it is the inexorable paradox of atheistic humanism. It is the drama of man being deprived of an essential dimension of his being—namely, his search for the infinite—and thus faced with having his being reduced in the worst way.

Thanks to the Gospel, the Church has the truth about man. This truth is found in an anthropology that the Church never ceases to fathom more thoroughly and to communicate to others. The primordial affirmation of this anthropology is that man is God's image and cannot be reduced to a mere portion of nature or a nameless element in the human city.

If the Church makes herself present in the defense of, or in the advancement of, man, she does so in line with her mission, which, although it is religious and not social or political, cannot fail to consider man in the entirety of his being. The Lord outlined in the parable of the Good Samaritan the model of attention to all human needs [Lk 10:29ff.], and he said that in the final analysis he will identify himself with the disinherited—the sick, the imprisoned, the hungry, the lonely—who have been given a helping hand [Mt 25:31ff.].

Let us also keep in mind that the Church's action in earthly mat-

ABOVE: *Releasing the dove of peace in Oaxaca.*

OPPOSITE: *Afternoon Mass at the Cathedral of Guadalupe.*

3

ters, such as human advancement, development, justice, and the rights of the individual, is always intended to be at the service of man—and of man as she sees him in the Christian vision of the anthropology that she adopts. She therefore does not need to have recourse to ideological systems in order to love, defend, and collaborate in the liberation of man; at the center of the message of which she is the depository and herald she finds inspiration for acting in favor of brotherhood, justice, and peace, against all forms of domination, slavery, discrimination, violence, attacks on religious liberty and aggression against man, and whatever attacks life.

There are many signs that help to distinguish when the liberation in question is Christian and when on the other hand it is based on ideologies that rob it of consistency with an evangelical view of man, of things, and of events. They are signs drawn from the content of what the evangelizers proclaim or from the concrete attitudes that they

A native dance group performs for the Pope.

Welcoming ceremony at Santo Domingo Airport.

adopt. At the level of content, one must see what is their fidelity to the word of God, to the Church's living tradition, and to her Magisterium. As for attitudes, one must consider what sense of communion they have with the Bishops, in the first place, and with the other sectors of the people of God; what contribution they make to the real building up of the community; in what form they lovingly show care for the poor, the sick, the dispossessed, the neglected, and the oppressed, and in what way they find in them the image of the poor and suffering Jesus, and strive to relieve their need and serve Christ in them.

Through you, Indians and peasants, there appears before me the immense multitude of the rural world, which is still the prevalent part of the Latin American continent and a very large sector, even nowadays, of our planet. . . .

The depressed rural world, the worker who, with his sweat, waters also his affliction, cannot wait any longer for full and effective recognition of his dignity, which is not inferior to that of any other social sector. He has the right to be respected and not to be deprived, maneuvers which are sometimes tantamount to real spoliation, of the little that he has. He has the right to be rid of the barriers of exploitation, often made up of intolerable selfishness, against which his best efforts of advancement are shattered. He has the right to real help—which is not charity or crumbs of justice—in order that he may have access to the development that his dignity as a man and as a son of God deserves.

Therefore it is necessary to act promptly and in depth. It is necessary to carry out bold changes, which are deeply innovative. It is necessary to undertake urgent reforms without waiting any longer.

It cannot be forgotten that the measures to be taken must be adequate. The Church does indeed defend the legitimate right to private property, but she also teaches no less clearly that there is always a social mortgage on all private property, in order that goods may serve the general purpose that God gave them. And if the common good requires it, there should be no hesitation even at expropriation, carried out in the due form.

The agricultural world has great importance and great dignity. It is just this world that offers society the products necessary for its nutrition. It is a task that deserves the appreciation and grateful esteem of all, which is a recognition of the dignity of those engaged in it; a dignity that can and must increase with the contemplation of God, contemplation encouraged by contact with nature, reflection of the divine action which looks after the grass in the fields, makes it grow, nourishes it; that makes the land fertile, sending it rain and wind, so that it may feed also animals, which help man, as we read at the beginning of Genesis.

Work in the fields involves great difficulties because of the effort it demands, the contempt with which it is sometimes considered, and the obstacles it meets with—difficulties which only a far-reaching action can solve. Otherwise, the flight from the countryside to the cities will continue, frequently creating problems of extensive and distressing proletarization, overcrowding in houses unworthy of human beings, and so on.

An evil that is quite widespread is the tendency to individualism among rural workers, whereas a better coordinated and united action could be of great help. Think of this too, dear sons.

The worker who, with his sweat, waters also his affliction, cannot wait any longer for full and effective recognition of his dignity . . . He has the right to real help—which is not charity or crumbs of justice.

POLAND

June 2 — 10, 1979

MAY 18

. . .

From the homily by Pope John Paul II at the Polish cemetery at Monte Cassino, Italy

Beloved Fellow Countrymen!

This is a special moment in which I can take part with you in the present great anniversary. Thirty-five years ago the battle for Monte Cassino ended—one of the decisive battles of the last war. For us who in that period had to bear the horrible oppression of the occupation, and for Poland, which found itself on the eve of the insurrection of Warsaw, that battle was a further confirmation of the inflexible will to live, of the fatherland's aspiration to independence, virtues which never for a moment abandoned us. At Monte Cassino the Polish soldier fought, here he fell, here he shed his blood, thinking of his country, of that country which is for us a beloved mother precisely because love for her demands sacrifice and hardship.

The inhabitants of this lovely country of Italy remember that the Polish soldier brought liberation to their country. They remember it

OPPOSITE: An interlude with Polish students.

LEFT: The Pope greeting a crowd at Gniezno.

OVERLEAF: John Paul II praying at his parents' tomb in Wadowice.

with esteem and love. We know that this soldier at the same time went by a long and tortuous route "from the land of Italy to Poland," as on a former occasion the legions of Dabrowski.

They were guided by the consciousness of a just cause, since a just cause was and shall never cease to be the right of a nation to existence and to independent existence, to social life in the spirit of its own national and religious convictions and traditions, and to the sovereignty of its own territory.

Many times have I walked in this cemetery. I have read the inscriptions on the stones giving for each one the date and place birth. These inscriptions brought before my mind's eye the features of my fatherland, of the country in which I was born. These inscriptions from so many places of the land of Poland, from all parts from the east to the west, from the south to the north, do not cease to cry out here in the heart of Europe, at the foot of the monastery which recalls the times of Saint Benedict, they do not cease to cry out as did the hearts of the soldiers who fought here.

O God, who protected Poland for so many centuries . . . we bow our heads before the heroes. Let us recommend their souls to God. Let us recommend to God the fatherland, Poland, Europe, the World.

OPPOSITE: *The cell of Saint Maximilian Kolbe at Auschwitz.*

BELOW: *The Pope praying at the Auschwitz Wall of the Dead.*

IRELAND

September 24 — October 1, 1979

Standing for the first time on Irish soil, on Armagh soil the Successor of Peter cannot but recall the first coming here, more than one thousand five hundred years ago, of Saint Patrick. From his days as a shepherd boy at Selmish right up to his death at Saul, Patrick was a witness to Jesus Christ. Not far from this spot, on the Hill of Slane, it is said that he lit, for the first time in Ireland, the Paschal Fire so that the light of Christ might shine forth on all of Ireland and unite all of its people in the love of the one Jesus Christ. It gives me great joy to stand here with you today, within sight of Slane, and to proclaim this same Jesus, the Incarnate Word of God, the Savior of the world. He is the Lord of history, the Light of the world, the Hope of the future of all humanity. In the words of the Easter Liturgy, celebrated for the first time in Ireland by Saint Patrick on the Hill of Slane, we greet Christ today: he is the Alpha and the Omega, the beginning of all things and their end. All time is his, and all the ages. To him be glory for ever and ever. *Lumen Christi: Deo Gratias.* The Light of Christ: Thanks be to God. May the light of Christ, the light of faith continue always to shine out from Ireland. May no darkness ever be able to extinguish it.

SEPTEMBER 29

· · ·

From John Paul II's address at Drogheda

Yes, Ireland, that has overcome so many difficult moments in her history, is being challenged in a new way today, for she is not immune to the influence of ideologies and trends which present-day civilization and progress carry with them. The very capability of mass media to bring the whole world into your homes produces a new kind of confrontation with values and trends that up until now have been

SEPTEMBER 29

· · ·

From Pope John Paul's homily in Phoenix Park, Dublin

alien to Irish society. Pervading materialism imposes its dominion on many today in many different forms and with an aggressiveness that spares no one. The most sacred principles, which were the sure guides for the behavior of individuals and society, are being hollowed out by false pretenses concerning freedom, the sacredness of life, the indissolubility of marriage, the true sense of human sexuality, the right attitude toward the material goods that progress has to offer. Many people now are tempted to self-indulgence and consumerism, and human identity is often defined by what one owns.

And so it becomes all the more urgent to steep ourselves in the truth that comes from Christ, "who is the way, the truth and the life" [Jn 14:6], and in the strength that he himself offers us through his Spirit. It is especially in the Eucharist that the power and the love of the Lord are given to us.

ABOVE: *Greeting an enthusiastic Irish crowd.*

OPPOSITE: *The Pope says farewell after celebrating Mass at Ballybrit racecourse.*

Every piece of art, be it religious or secular, be it a painting, a sculpture, a poem, or any form of handicraft made by loving skill, is a sign and a symbol of the inscrutable secret of human existence.

Praying at Saint Patrick's grave.

This visit to Clonmacnois gives me the opportunity to render homage to the traditions of faith and Christian living in Ireland.

In particular, I wish to recall and honor the great monastic contribution to Ireland that was made here on this revered spot for one thousand years, and whose influence was carried all over Europe by missionary monks and by students of this monastic school of Clonmacnois.

Clonmacnois was long the center of a renowned school of sacred art. The Shrine of Saint Manchan, standing on the altar today, is one outstanding example of its work. This is therefore a fitting place for me to express my gratitude for the works of Irish sacred art, several pieces of which have been presented to me on the occasion of my visit.

Irish art embodies in many instances the deep faith and devotion of the Irish people as expressed in the personal sensitivity of its artists. Every piece of art, be it religious or secular, be it a painting, a sculpture, a poem, or any form of handicraft made by loving skill, is a sign and a symbol of the inscrutable secret of human existence, of man's origin and destiny, of the meaning of his life and work. It speaks to us of the meaning of birth and death, of the greatness of man.

Praised be Jesus Christ!

Here I am at the goal of my journey to Ireland: the Shrine of Our Lady at Knock. Since I first learned of the centenary of this shrine, which is being celebrated this year, I have felt a strong desire to come here, the desire to make yet another pilgrimage to the Shrine of the Mother of Christ, the Mother of the Church, the Queen of Peace. Do not be surprised at this desire of mine. It has been my custom to make pilgrimages to the shrines of Our Lady, starting with my earliest youth and in my own country. I made such pilgrimages also as a Bishop and as a Cardinal. I know very well that every people, every country, indeed every diocese, has its holy places in which the heart of the whole people of God beats, one could say, in more lively fashion: places of special encounter between God and human beings; places in which Christ dwells in a special way in our midst. If these places are so often dedicated to his Mother, it reveals all the more fully to us the nature of his Church. Since the Second Vatican Council, which concluded its

Greeting the faithful at Galway Airport.

Constitution on the Church with the chapter on "The Blessed Virgin Mary, Mother of God, in the Mystery of Christ and of the Church," this fact is more evident for us today than ever—yes, for all of us, for all Christians. Do we not confess with all our brethren, even with those with whom we are not yet linked in full unity, that we are a pilgrim people? As once this people traveled on its pilgrimage under the guidance of Moses, so we, the people of God of the New Covenant, are traveling on our pilgrim way under the guidance of Christ.

I am here, then, as a pilgrim, a sign of the pilgrim Church throughout the world participating, through my presence as Peter's Successor, in a very special way in the centenary celebration of this shrine.

THE
UNITED STATES
October 1 — 7, 1979

Tonight, in a very special way, I hold out my hands to the youth of America. In Mexico City and Guadalajara I met the youth of Latin America. In Warsaw and Krakow I met the youth of Poland. In Rome I meet frequently groups of young people from Italy and from all over the world. Yesterday I met the youth of Ireland in Galway. And now with great joy I meet you. For me, each one of these meetings is a new discovery. Again and again I find in young people the joy and enthusiasm of life, a searching for truth and for the deeper meaning of the existence that unfolds before them in all its attraction and potential.

Tonight I want to repeat what I keep telling youth: You are the future of the world, and "the day of tomorrow belongs to you."

OCTOBER 1

. . .

*From the Pope's homily on Boston
Common*

Social thinking and social practice inspired by the Gospel must always be marked by a special sensitivity toward those who are most in distress, those who are extremely poor, those suffering from all the physical, mental, and moral ills that afflict humanity, including hunger, neglect, unemployment, and despair. There are many poor people of this sort around the world. There are many in your own midst. On many occasions, your nation has gained a well-deserved reputation for generosity, both public and private. Be faithful to that tradition, in keeping with your vast possibility and present responsibilities. The network of charitable works of each kind that the

OCTOBER 2

. . . .

*From the homily delivered by Pope John
Paul II in Yankee Stadium, New York*

*The Pope delivering a homily in
front of the Capitol building,
Washington, D.C.*

Church has succeeded in creating here is a valuable means for effectively mobilizing generous undertakings aimed at relieving the situations of distress that continually arise both at home and elsewhere in the world. Make an effort to ensure that this form of aid keeps its irreplaceable character as a fraternal and personal encounter with those who are in distress; if necessary, reestablish this very character against all the elements that work in the opposite direction. Let this sort of aid be respectful of the freedom and dignity of those being helped, and let it be a means of forming the conscience of the givers.

But this is not enough. Within the framework of your national institutions and in cooperation with all of your compatriots, you will also want to seek out the structural causes of the different forms of

ABOVE: *The Pope at Boston Cathedral.*

OPPOSITE: *The Pontifex Maximus addressing the United Nations General Assembly.*

The poor of the United States and of the world are your brothers and sisters in Christ. . . . You must take of your substance, and not just of your abundance, in order to help them.

His Holiness in Chicago.

poverty in the world and in your own country, so that you can apply the proper remedies. You will not allow yourselves to be intimidated or discouraged by oversimplified explanations, which are more ideological than scientific explanations and which try to account for a complex evil by some single cause. But neither will you recoil before the reforms—even profound ones—of attitudes and structures that may prove necessary in order to re-create over and over again the conditions needed by the disadvantaged if they are to have a fresh chance in the hard struggle of life. The poor of the United States and of the world are your brothers and sisters in Christ. You must never be content to leave them just the crumbs from the feast. You must take of your substance, and not just of your abundance, in order to help them. And you must treat them like guests at your family table.

The parable of the rich man and Lazarus must always be present in our memory; it must form our conscience. Christ demands openness to our brothers and sisters in need—openness from the rich, the affluent, the economically advanced; openness to the poor, the under-developed, and the disadvantaged. Christ demands an openness that is more than benign attention, more than token actions or halfhearted efforts that leave the poor as destitute as before, or even more so.

All of humanity must think of the parable of the rich man and the beggar. Humanity must translate it in contemporary terms, in terms of economy and politics, in terms of all human rights, in terms of relations between the First, Second, and Third Worlds. We cannot stand idly by when thousands of human beings are dying of hunger. Nor can we remain indifferent when the rights of the human spirit are trampled upon, when violence is done to the human conscience in matters of truth, religion, and cultural creativity.

We cannot stand idly by, enjoying our own riches and freedom, if, in any place, the Lazarus of the twentieth century stands at our doors. In the light of the parable of Christ, riches and freedom mean a special responsibility.

The Pope on his way to celebrate Mass at Yankee Stadium.

LEFT: *Fifth Avenue, New York City.*

OPPOSITE: *On the steps of St. Patrick's Cathedral, New York City.*

You who are farmers today are stewards of a gift from God which was intended for the good of all humanity. You have the potential to provide food for the millions who have nothing to eat and thus help to rid the world of famine.

Recall the time when Jesus saw the hungry crowd gathered on the hillside. What was his response? He did not content himself with expressing his compassion. He gave his disciples the command, "Give them something to eat yourselves" [Mt 14:16]. Did He not intend those same words for us today, for us who live at the closing of the twentieth century, for us who have the means available to feed the hungry of the world?

OCTOBER 4

· · ·

From the address by Pope John Paul II to the rural community of St. Patrick Parish in Des Moines, Iowa

TURKEY

November 28 — 30, 1979

I am happy at this opportunity given to me to manifest my esteem of the Turkish people. As I already knew and as I have experienced in these days, it is a nation rightly proud of itself, which intends to solve its political, economic, and social problems in dignity, democracy, and independence. It is rich in very large numbers of young people, and it is resolved to use all the resources of modern progress. I express cordial good wishes for its future.

I could not help meditating on its past also. For millennia—it is possible to go back at least to the Hittites—this country has been a crossroads and a melting pot of civilizations, at the junction of Asia and Europe. How many cultural riches are buried, not only in its archeological remains and its venerable monuments, but in the soul, in the more or less conscious memory of its people! How many adventures, too, glorious or challenging, have formed the web of its history!

The meeting takes place locally but it is connected geographically according to the ecclesiastical formulation with the whole West and East—and according to the modern geographical formulation of ecumenism it is connected also with the North and the South.

The meeting takes place today, but it is connected with the distant past, the past of the common Apostles, the common Fathers, the common Martyrs and Confessors, the Ecumenical Councils, concelebration on the same altar, and communion in the same chalice.

The Pope of the West meets the Metropolitan of the East.

LEFT: *Celebrating Mass at Istanbul's Church of the Holy Spirit.*

BELOW: *Pope John Paul II visits a tomb at Ephesus.*

AFRICA

May 2 — 12, 1980

Men are thirsty for love, for brotherly charity, but there are also whole peoples who are thirsty for the water necessary for their life, in special circumstances which are present in my mind, now that I am among you, in this land of Upper Volta, in this area of Sahel. If the problem of the progressive advance of the desert arises also in other regions of the globe, the sufferings of the people of Sahel, which the world has witnessed, invite me to speak of it here.

Human solidarity must be manifested to come to the help of the victims and the countries which cannot cope at once with so many urgent needs, and the economy of which may be ruined. It is a ques-

MAY 11

From Pope John Paul II's speech in
Ouagadougou, Upper Volta

OPPOSITE: *Accepting gifts in Kenya.*

LEFT: *The Pope performs a marriage ceremony in Kumasi, Ghana.*

Men are thirsty for love,
for brotherly charity, but
there are also whole
peoples who are thirsty
for the water necessary for
their life.

Greeting the faithful in Zaire.

tion of international justice, especially with regard to countries that are too often overtaken by these disasters, whereas others are in geographical or climatic conditions which must, in comparison, be called privileged. It is also a question of charity for all those who consider that every man and woman is a brother and a sister whose sufferings must be borne and alleviated by everyone. Solidarity, in justice and charity, must know no frontiers or limits.

From here, from Ouagadougou, the center of one of these countries that can be called the countries of thirst, allow me, therefore, to make a solemn appeal to all, in Africa and beyond this continent, not to close their eyes to what has happened and is happening in the region of Sahel.

Today, therefore, let us thank all those who dedicated themselves, all those who came to the help of their brothers in need. May they hear the Lord say to them one day: "I was thirsty and you gave me drink" [Mt 25:35].

ABOVE: *The Pope listens to a native band in Upper Volta.*

RIGHT: *Praying at Kisangani.*

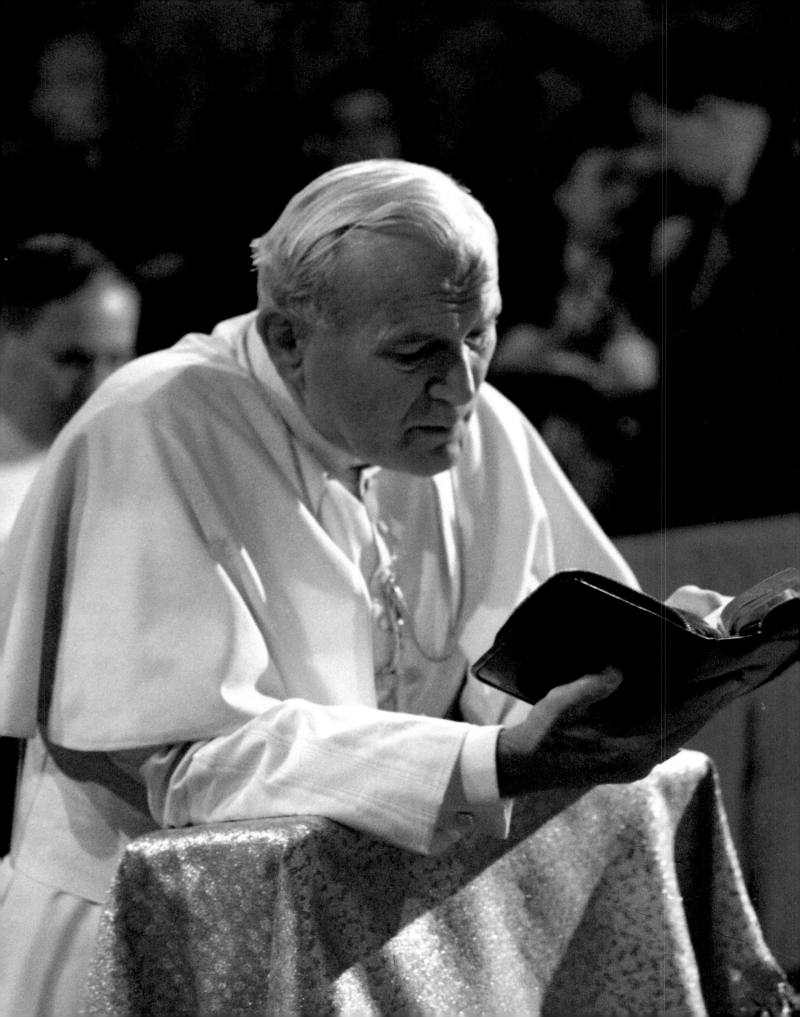

FRANCE

May 30 — June 12, 1980

I know that in this assembly it is mainly workers who are listening to me. Today this district, around its ancient basilica, has become one of the most working-class districts in the Parisian suburbs. And I know that many workers, Frenchmen and foreigners, live and work here, often under precarious conditions as regards housing, wages, and jobs. I think also of the French population from beyond the seas. An important number of their sons work here, in Paris.

Yes, this present-day urban life makes human relations difficult, in the hectic rush, never ending, between the place of work, the family lodging, and the shopping centers. The integration of the children, of the young, of the old, often raises acute problems. There are so many appeals to work together to create more and more human conditions of life for everyone!

Our modern world witnesses the increase of the terrible threat of the destruction of men by other men, especially with the accumulation of nuclear weapons. Already the cost of these weapons and the threatening atmosphere they bring about have caused millions of men and entire populations to see reduced their possibilities of bread and of freedom. Under these conditions, the great society of workers, precisely in the name of the moral power with which it is endowed, must demand categorically and clearly: Where, in what field, why, have the bounds of this noble struggle been overstepped, the struggle for the good of man, in particular the most underprivileged and the neediest? Where, in what field, why, has this moral and creative power been turned into a destructive force, hatred, in the new forms of collective selfishness in which glimpses can be caught of the threat of . . . a struggle of all against all, and of a monstrous self-destruction?

MAY 31

· · ·

From the Pope's homily at Saint-Denis, Paris

ABOVE: *The Pope after celebrating Mass at Lisieux.*

43

BRAZIL

June 30 — July 11, 1980

The Church all over the world wishes to be the Church of the poor. Also, the Church of Brazil wishes to be the Church of the poor, that is, she wishes to extract all the truth contained in the Beatitudes of Christ and especially in this first one: "Blessed are the poor in spirit. . . ." She wishes to teach this truth and she wishes to put it into practice, just as Jesus came to do and to teach.

The Church of the poor says the same, with greater forcefulness, to those who have more than they need, who live in abundance, who live in luxury. She says to them: Just look around a little! Doesn't your heart ache? Do you not feel remorse of conscience owing to your riches and abundance? If not, if you only want to have more and more, if your idol is profit and pleasure, remember that man's value is not

JULY 10

· · ·

From the Pope's address to the Indians of Amazonia

OPPOSITE: *The Pope with his Secretary of State, Cardinal Caseroli, and Brazilian bishops.*

OVERLEAF: *John Paul II reaches out to performers at Belo Horizonte.*

The Pope praying at the cathedral in Brasilia.

measured by what he has, but by what he *is*. So let him who has accumulated a great deal, and who thinks that everything is summed up in this, remember that he may be worth far less (within himself and in the eyes of God) than any of those poor and unknown persons.

The measure of riches, of money, and of luxury is not equivalent to the measure of the real dignity of a man.

The Church of the poor speaks, therefore, to man—to each man and to all. At the same time she speaks to societies, to societies in their totality and to the various special strata, to different groups and professions. She also speaks to systems and to social, socioeconomic, and sociopolitical structures. She speaks the language of the Gospel, explaining it also in the light of the progress of human science, but without introducing extraneous, heterodox elements, contrary to its spirit. She speaks to all in the name of Christ and she speaks also in the name of man (especially to those for whom the name of Christ does not mean everything, does not express the whole truth about man that this name contains). . . .

The Church of the poor speaks, consequently, as follows: Do everything, you particularly who have decision-making powers, you on whom the situation of the world depends, do everything so that the life of every man in your country may become more human, more worthy of man!

Do everything in order that there may disappear, at least gradually, that abyss which separates the excessively rich, few in number, from the great crowds of the poor, of those who live in want. Do everything so that this abyss may not increase but be reduced, that social equality may be aimed at, that the unjust distribution of goods may make way for a more just distribution.

Do it out of consideration for every man who is your neighbor and your fellow citizen. Do it out of consideration for the common good of all. And do it also out of consideration for yourselves. Only a society that is socially just, that endeavors to be more and more just, has a *raison d'être*. Only such a society has a future before it. A society that is not just, on the social plane, and does not aim at becoming such, endangers its own future. Think, therefore, of the past, and look to the present and plan a better future for your whole society!

All this is contained in what Christ said in the Sermon on the Mount, in the content of this one sentence: "Blessed are the poor in spirit, for theirs is the kingdom of heaven."

Dear brothers and sisters, with this message I renew my sentiments of deep affection, and as a token of abundant graces from God I leave you and your families my Apostolic Blessing.

I entrust to the public authorities and to others in positions of responsibility the wishes that, in this meeting with you, I make from the bottom of my heart in the Lord's name: that you, whose ancestors were the first inhabitants of this land, having a special right to it throughout the generations, should be recognized as having the right to inhabit it in peace and serenity without the fear—a real nightmare—of being turned out for the benefit of others, but instead sure of a vital space not only for your survival, but also for the preservation of your identity as a human group, as a real people, and a nation.

Serenaded by a choir after celebrating Mass.

Yes, from the top of these mountains there is no one who cannot contemplate [Christ's] image, in an attitude of welcome and embrace, and imagine him as he is, always ready to meet man, and eager, too, that man should come toward him. Now this is the only motive that the Church—and with her the Pope at this moment—has before her eyes and in her heart: that every man may meet Christ in order that Christ may walk with every man along the ways of life.

A symbol of love, a call to reconciliation and an invitation to brotherhood, here Christ the Redeemer proclaims continually the power of truth over man and over the world. . . .

At this moment, illuminated by Christ's glance, the Pope's eyes turn to every inhabitant of this metropolis, and the Pope's voice, a mere echo and resonance of Christ's voice, would like to speak, from heart to heart, to one and all. He would like, as in a short visit, to reach every home and also those who do not have one: meeting places and places of work, where there is joy but also where there is suffering, especially where there is pain and sorrow—hospitals, prisons, the ways of the homeless, the hungry, of those bereft of love.

JULY 10

· · ·

From John Paul II's address at
Corcavado in Rio de Janeiro

ABOVE: *John Paul II being welcomed by*
the inhabitants of Curitiba.

OPPOSITE: *John Paul II joyously greeting*
the masses at Belo Horizonte.

From the top of these mountains there is no one who cannot contemplate [Christ's] image, in an attitude of welcome and embrace, and imagine him as he is, always ready to meet man, and eager, too, that man should come toward him.

The Pope in a cable car above Rio de Janeiro.

GERMANY

November 15 — 19, 1980

The history of the relationship between the Church, on the one hand, and art in architecture, the visual arts, literature, the theater, and music, on the other, has been eventful. If it had not been for the efforts of the monasteries, for instance, the treasures of ancient Greek and Latin authors would doubtless not have been handed down to us. At that time the Church showed great candor in its dialogue with ancient literature and culture. For a long time the Church was considered the mother of the arts. It was the Church which commissioned art. The contents of the Christian faith determined the motifs and themes of art. How true this is can easily be demonstrated by stopping to think what would remain if one removed everything connected with religious and Christian inspiration from European and German art history.

In recent centuries, most strongly since about 1800, the connection between the Church and culture, and thus between the Church and art, has grown more tenuous.

The question arises: Where are the mutual connections between the Church and art, the Church and journalism? The answer to this is: the subject of the Church and the subject of both artists and journalists is man, the image of man, the truth of man, the *ecce homo*, including his history, his world and environment, as well as the social, economic, and political context.

Today, literature, the theater, film, and the visual arts see their function largely in terms of criticism, protest, opposition, and pointing an accusing finger at existing conditions. The beautiful as a category of art seems to have fallen by the wayside in favor of depictions of man in his negative aspects, in his contradictions, in his hopelessness, and in the absence of meaning. This seems to be the current *ecce homo*. The so-called intact world is an object of scorn and cynicism.

OPPOSITE: *His Holiness in the
"Popemobile" in Mainz.*

The Christian faith and the Christian Church do not object to the depiction of evil in its various forms. Evil is a reality whose extent has been experienced and suffered in this century in the extreme by your country and mine. Without the reality of evil, the reality of good, redemption, mercy, and salvation cannot be measured. This is not a license for evil, but rather an indication of its position.

Helping, healing, purging, and purifying power was ascribed to art by the Greeks. There should be encouragement for hope and the attempt to find meaning in life, even though not all questions as to the whys and wherefores of human existence can be answered. All this must not be lost in modern art, for its own sake and for the sake of man. In this service to man there can be and should be a connection between the Church and art, without the need for either side to lose any of its own identity.

ABOVE: *Midnight Mass at Altottino.*

OPPOSITE: *The Pope praying at the tomb of Saint Albert in Fuldeon.*

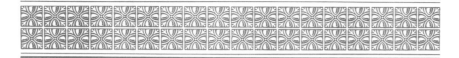

THE PHILIPPINES
AND GUAM

February 17 — 23, 1981

First and foremost, be genuine young people. What is it to be young? To be young means possessing within oneself an incessant newness of spirit, nourishing a continual quest for good, and persevering in reaching a goal. Being genuinely young in this sense is the way to prepare for your future, which is to fulfill your vocation as fully mature adults. Never try to ignore, then, the irresistable force that is driving you toward the future.

The Church is not frightened by the intensity of your feelings. It is a sign of vitality. It indicates pent-up energy, which of itself is neither good nor bad, but can be used for good causes or for bad. It is

FEBRUARY 19

· · ·

From the Pope's address to students of Pontifical University of St. Thomas, Manila

BELOW: *The people of Manila greet the Pope.*

First and foremost,
be genuine young
people. . . . The Church is
not frightened by the
intensity of your feelings.

ABOVE: *The Pope and Mother Teresa in Manila.*

RIGHT: *John Paul II blessing children at Marong.*

The Pope celebrating Mass at an improvised altar in Guam.

like rainwater that accumulates on the mountains after days and days of raining. When whatever holds it bursts, it unleashes forces capable of wiping whole towns off the map, overwhelming their inhabitants in a sea of tears and blood. But if the water is properly channeled, dry fields are irrigated, producing necessary food and much-needed energy. In your case it is not only food or material things that are involved; it is the destiny of your country, the future of your generation, and the security of children yet unborn. It is without any doubt an exciting but crucial challenge for you, my dear young people. And I am positive that you can meet this challenge, that you are willing to assume this responsibility—above all, that you are ready to prepare yourselves now, today.

Yes, human dignity must be promoted by the land. Because the land is a gift of God for the benefit of all, it is not permissible to use this gift in such a manner that the benefits it produces serve only a limited number of people, while the others—the vast majority—are excluded from the benefits that the land yields.

A truly Christian challenge is therefore presented to those who own or control the land. I know that many of you who are plantation owners or who are planters are truly concerned with the welfare of your workers, but the Church, aware of her responsibilities, feels impelled to hold up before you again and again the ideal of love and justice, and to encourage you to compare constantly your actions and attitudes with the ethical principles regarding the priority of the common good and regarding the social purpose of economic activity. The right of ownership is legitimate in itself but it cannot be separated from its wider social dimension. In his encyclical *Populorum Progressio*, Paul VI, echoing the teaching of the Second Vatican Council, stated this principle very clearly when he wrote: "God intended the earth and all it contains for the use of every human being and people. Thus, as all people follow justice and unite in charity, created goods should abound for them on a reasonable basis."

From the Pope's address to proprietors and workers of Bacolod City, Philippines

John Paul II celebrating outdoor Mass at Iloilo.

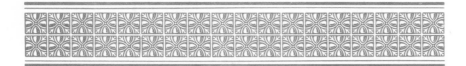

JAPAN

February 23 — 26, 1981

You also asked me a question about music. I cannot play any musical instrument. I have never actively devoted myself to this branch of the art of music. But I have a deep feeling for the beauty of music and I am very fond of singing. I have spent many hours (especially during my vacations) singing with young people. Even now, during the vacation period, various groups of young people come to Castel Gandolfo and sing. I hope that one day you will also come, although I realize that it is a long way for you to travel.

One of my reasons for coming to Japan was in order to stop at Hiroshima, at the place where the first atomic bomb exploded, an event that represents a terrible warning. As I read the material which you sent, I noted that you were deeply concerned about the problem of peace—a true peace—as is right and natural, especially after the experience of 1945. In your statements you note that peace cannot be based only on a balance of weaponry, that it cannot take the dominance of the strong over the weak as its presupposition, and that it cannot go hand in hand with any sort of imperialism.

The Church thinks in the same way as you do and teaches in the same way.

These are the themes of my peace messages: in 1979, "To reach peace, teach peace"; in 1980, "Truth, the power of peace"; in 1981, "To serve peace, respect freedom."

Peace must be built above all by those who are responsible for international decisions. However, they must bear in mind—as the Church keeps reminding us—that peace means, in the first place, a true order in the relationships between individuals and nations. Thus the building of peace from its foundations ought to mean recognizing and so respecting all human rights, whether they concern the

From John Paul II's dialogue with Japanese youth at Budokan, Tokyo

John Paul II sings with Japanese children performing a ritual dance.

War is the work of man.

War is destruction of

human life. War is death.

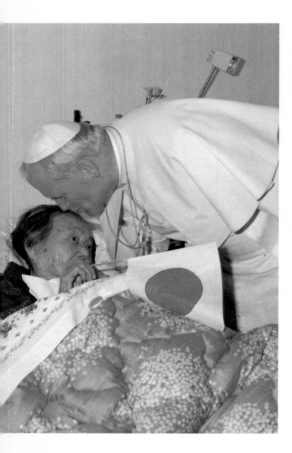

ABOVE: *The Pope blesses a Nagasaki bomb victim.*

RIGHT: *Praying at the Hiroshima Memorial.*

material aspect or the spiritual dimension of our earthly existence, and respecting the rights of all nations, without exception, whether large or small. Peace cannot exist if the great and powerful violate the rights of the weak.

War is the work of man. War is destruction of human life. War is death.

Nowhere do these truths impose themselves upon us more forcefully than in this city of Hiroshima, at this Peace Memorial. Two cities will forever have their names linked together, two Japanese cities, Hiroshima and Nagasaki, as the only cities in the world that have had the ill fortune to be a reminder that man is capable of destruction beyond belief. Their names will forever stand out as the names of the only cities in our time that have been singled out as a warning to future generations that war can destroy human efforts to build a world of peace.

To remember the past is to commit oneself to the future. To re-

FEBRUARY 25

. . .

From John Paul II's address at the Peace Memorial, Hiroshima

member Hiroshima is to abhor nuclear war. To remember Hiroshima is to commit oneself to peace. To remember what the people of this city suffered is to renew our faith in man, in his capacity to do what is good, in his freedom to choose what is right, in his determination to turn disaster into a new beginning. In the face of the man-made calamity that every war is, one must affirm and reaffirm, again and again, that the waging of war is not inevitable or unchangeable. Humanity is not destined to self-destruction. Clashes of ideologies, aspirations, and needs can and must be settled and resolved by means other than war and violence. Humanity owes it to itself to settle differences and conflicts by peaceful means.

Ladies and gentlemen, you who devote your lives to the modern sciences, you are the first to be able to evaluate the disaster that a nuclear war would inflict on the human family. And I know that, ever since the explosion of the first atomic bomb, many of you have been anxiously wondering about the responsibility of modern science and of the technology that is the fruit of that science. In a number of countries, associations of scholars and research workers express the anxiety of the scientific world in the face of an irresponsible use of science, which too often does grievous damage to the balance of nature, or brings with it the ruin and oppression of man by man. One thinks in the first place of physics, chemistry, biology, and the genetic sciences, of which you rightly condemn those applications or experimentations which are detrimental to humanity. But one also has in mind the social sciences and the human behavioral sciences when they are utilized to manipulate people, to crush their minds, souls, dignity, and freedom. Criticism of science and technology is sometimes so severe that it comes close to condemning science itself. On the contrary, science and technology are wonderful products of a God-given human creativity, since they have provided us with wonderful possibilities, and we all gratefully benefit from them. But we know that this potential is not a neutral one; it can be used either for man's progress or for his degradation. Like you, I have lived through this period, which I would call the "post-Hiroshima period," and I share your anxieties. And today I feel inspired to say this to you: Surely the time has come for our society, and especially for the world of science, to realize that the future of humanity depends, as never before, on our collective moral choices.

FEBRUARY 25

. . .

From the speech by John Paul II to scientists and representatives of the United Nations University, Tokyo

Surrounded by Japanese women in ceremonial dress.

AFRICA

February 12 — 19, 1982

I would now like to direct my words to those members of the Church in Nigeria who are industrialists and workers, employers and employees. You are playing a vital role in the life of your nation, and people expect much of you. The Church, too, looks to you with great hope.

People who work enjoy a God-given dignity. God could have created everything on earth in its final form, but he decided differently. For God wants us to be associated with him in the improvement of the things he has made. By our work we share in God's own creative activity. It was the same with Christ himself in his human nature.

Work is also man's way of helping his neighbor. One person's work affects another person, and together workers help to build up the whole of society. Those who work can say: When we work conscientiously, we make a real contribution toward a better world. Our work is an act of solidarity with our brothers and sisters.

Between employers and employees there can sometimes arise cases of misunderstanding. These are to be resolved, not by violence, harsh words, and antagonisms, but by mutual respect, willingness to listen, and patient dialogue. Workers have the right to form unions and to ask for proper working conditions. But they also have the obligation to render loyal service, and employers have the right to receive the services for which they pay. Workers should not too readily have recourse to strikes, which generally cause much suffering to many; strikes remain extraordinary measures for the defense of human rights.

Do nothing to sabotage the economy of your own country. Nothing can replace diligent, efficient, and honest hard work on your part.

FEBRUARY 16

From John Paul II's homily for workers at Holy Cross Cathedral, Lagos, Nigeria

ABOVE: *The Vicar of Christ pays homage to the Cross.*

OPPOSITE: *The Pope's arrival at Onitsha.*

PORTUGAL

May 12 — 15, 1982

Culture is of man, begins from man, and is for man.

   Culture is *of* man. In the past, when one wanted to define man, almost always one referred to intelligence, freedom, or language. Recent progress in cultural and philosophical anthropology demonstrates that it is possible to obtain a no less precise definition of human reality by referring to culture. This characterizes man and distinguishes him from other beings no less clearly than do intelligence, freedom, and language.

   Culture comes *from* man. He receives freely from nature a group of abilities—talents, as they are called in the Gospel—and with his intelligence, his willpower, and his work, he must develop them and make them bear fruit. The development of his own talents, as much on the part of the individual as on the part of a social group, with the aim of perfecting himself and subduing nature, builds up culture.

   Understood in this way, culture embraces the totality of the life of a people: a set of values which animates it and which, being shared by all its citizens, unites them in one "personal and collective conscience."

MAY 15

. . .

*From the discourse by Pope John Paul II
at the University of Coimbra*

OPPOSITE: *Praying to Our Lady of Fatima.*

LEFT: *The Pope in Lisbon.*

E N G L A N D

May 28 — June 2, 1982

My dear brothers and sisters of the Anglican Communion, "whom I love and long for" [Phil 4:1], how happy I am to be able to speak directly to you today in this great cathedral! The building itself is an eloquent witness both to our long years of common inheritance and to the sad years of division that followed. Beneath this roof Saint Thomas Becket suffered martyrdom. Here too we recall Augustine and Dunstan and Anselm and all those monks who gave such diligent service in this church. The great events of salvation history are retold in the ancient stained glass windows above us. And we have venerated here the manuscript of the Gospels sent from Rome to Canterbury thirteen hundred years ago. Encouraged by the witness of so many who have professed their faith in Jesus Christ through the cen-

MAY 29

. . .

From the Pope's address at Canterbury Cathedral

OPPOSITE: *John Paul II and the Archbishop of Canterbury leaving Westminster Abbey.*

LEFT: *The Pope and the Archbishop of Canterbury join in an ecumenical ceremony.*

turies, often at the cost of their own lives—a sacrifice which even to-day is asked of not a few, as the new chapel we shall visit reminds us—I appeal to you in this holy place, all my fellow Christians, and especially the members of the Church of England and the members of the Anglican Communion throughout the world, to accept the commitment to which Archbishop Runcie and I pledge ourselves anew before you today. This commitment is that of praying and working for reconciliation and ecclesial unity according to the mind and heart of our Savior Jesus Christ.

ABOVE: *The Pope celebrating Mass in London.*

RIGHT: *An outdoor Mass for thousands at Wembley Stadium.*

We are close to the city of Coventry, a city devastated by war but re-built in hope. The ruins of the old cathedral and the building of the new are recognized throughout the world as a symbol of Christian reconciliation and peace. We pray at this Mass: "Send forth your Spirit, O Lord, and renew the face of the earth." In this prayer we call upon God to enable us to bring about that reconciliation and peace not simply in symbol, but in reality too.

Our world is disfigured by war and violence. The ruins of the old cathedral constantly remind our society of its capacity to destroy. And today that capacity is greater than ever. People are having to live un-der the shadow of a nuclear nightmare. Yet people everywhere long for peace. Men and women of goodwill desire to make common cause in their search for a worldwide community of brotherhood and un-derstanding. They long for justice, yes, but for justice filled with mercy. Being so close to Shakespeare's birthplace, we would do well to consider this: "that in the course of justice none of us should see salvation. We do pray for mercy, and that same prayer doth teach us all to render the deeds of mercy."

What is this peace for which we long? What is this peace symbol-ized by the new cathedral of Coventry? Peace is not just the absence

MAY 30
. . .
From the Pope's address at Coventry

ABOVE: *The Pope celebrates a special Mass for priests and nuns in Coventry.*

of war. It involves mutual respect and confidence between peoples and nations. It involves collaboration and binding agreements. Like a cathedral, peace has to be constructed, patiently and with unshakable faith.

Wherever the strong exploit the weak, wherever the rich take advantage of the poor, wherever great powers seek to dominate and to impose ideologies, there the work of making peace is undone; there the cathedral of peace is again destroyed. Today, the scale and the horror of modern warfare—whether nuclear or not—makes it totally unacceptable as a means of settling differences between nations. War should belong to the tragic past, to history; it should find no place on humanity's agenda for the future.

There is an episode in the life of Saint Andrew, the patron saint of Scotland, that can serve as an example for what I wish to tell you. Jesus had been teaching a crowd of five thousand people about the Kingdom of God. They had listened carefully all day, and as evening approached he did not want to send them away hungry, so he told his disciples to give them something to eat. He said this really to test them, because he knew exactly what he was going to do. One of the disciples—it was Saint Andrew—said: "There is a small boy here with five barley loaves and two fishes; but what is that between so many?" Jesus took the loaves, blessed them, and gave them out to all who were sitting waiting; he then did the same with the fish, giving out as much as was wanted. Later the disciples collected twelve baskets of the fragments that were left over [Jn 6:1–14].

Now the point I wish to make is this: Saint Andrew gave Jesus all there was available, and Jesus miraculously fed those five thousand people and still had something left over. It is exactly the same with your lives. Left alone to face the difficult challenges of life today, you feel conscious of your inadequacy and afraid of what the future may hold for you. But what I say to you is this: *Place your lives in the hands of Jesus.* He will accept you, and bless you, and he will make such use of your lives as will be beyond your greatest expectations! In other words: surrender yourselves, like so many loaves and fishes, into the all-powerful, sustaining hands of God and you will find yourselves transformed with "newness of life" [Rom 6:4], with fullness of life [Jn 1:16]. "Unload your burden on the Lord, and he will support you" [Ps 55:22].

MAY 31

· · ·

From His Holiness' speech to youth at Murrayfield Stadium, Edinburgh

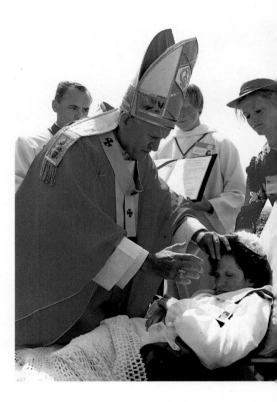

A Pastoral blessing for the infirm.

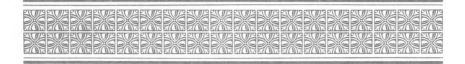

ARGENTINA

June 11 — 12, 1982

True and lasting peace must be the mature fruit of achieved integration of patriotism and universality.

Unite yourself also with the youth of Great Britain, who during these last days applauded and were equally sensitive to every prayer for peace and harmony. In this regard, with true joy I pass on to you a message I received for you. They themselves asked, above all, during the meeting in Cardiff, that I bring to you their sincere desire for peace.

Do not allow hate to lessen the generous energies and the capacity to come to terms with everyone, which you have within yourselves. With joined hands—together with Latin-American youth, who in

From the Pope's address to the Episcopal Conference in Buenos Aires

OPPOSITE: *Delivering a homily at the cathedral of Buenos Aires.*

BELOW: *Paying reverence to the Mother of God.*

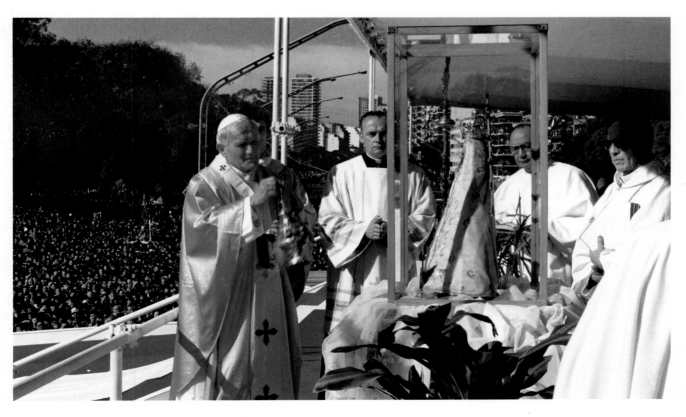

Puebla entrusted themselves to the special care of the Church—make a chain of union stronger than the chains of war. In this way you will be young preparers of a better future world; in this way you will be Christians.

From this place, where with the hymn of the great Eucharistic Congress you beseeched the God of hearts to teach love to all nations, now from this place, may there be kindled, in every Argentine heart throughout society, love, respect for each person, understanding, and peace.

Amen.

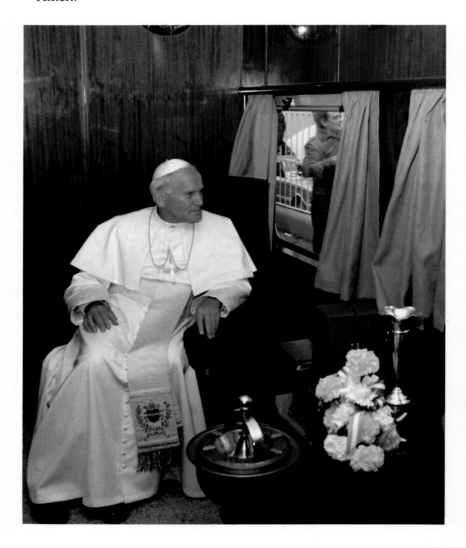

RIGHT: *The Pope at the altar of the Virgin Mary.*

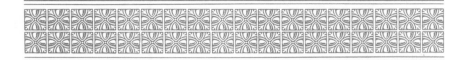

SPAIN

October 31 — November 9, 1982

Our faith teaches us that the Holy Eucharist constitutes the greatest gift which Christ has offered and permanently offers to his Spouse. It is at the root and is the summit of the Christian life and of all of the Church's activity. It is our greatest treasure, which contains "all of the spiritual good of the Church." . . . She must zealously look after what refers to this mystery and affirm it in its integrity as the heart and proof of that authentic spiritual renovation that was proposed by the last Council.

In this consecrated Host are summed up the words of Christ, his handing over his life to the Father for us, and the glory of his risen body. In the hours you spend before the sacred Host you have realized that this presence of Emmanuel, God-with-us, is at the same time

NOVEMBER 1

. . .

From the homily by John Paul II at the Mass celebrated in the "Mexican Parish" of Guadalupe, in Madrid

OPPOSITE: *Conversing with the Bishop of Santiago de Campostela.*

LEFT: *Homage at the altar of the Virgin Mary in Montserrat.*

I come as a messenger of peace, as a sustainer of hope, as a servant of faith, to strengthen the faithful in their fidelity to Christ and to his Church.

From the Pope's discourse at Managua Airport, Nicaragua, March 4, 1983.

ABOVE: *Burning incense preparatory to Mass.*

RIGHT: *Celebrating Mass at Loyola.*

a mystery of faith, a pledge of hope, and the wellspring of love for God and among men.

It is a mystery of faith because the crucified and risen Lord is really present in the Eucharist; not only during the celebration of the Holy Sacrifice, but as he subsists in the sacramental species.

I know that I have come to a nation of a great Catholic tradition, many of whose people have contributed immensely to the civilization and evangelization of other peoples. It is a history which speaks highly of your past.

Today you are committed to a restructuring of your political order, one which will rightly respect the unity and particularity of the diverse peoples who make up the nation. Without claiming to make concrete judgments on aspects which are not within my competence, I ask God to enlighten you on the choice of solutions so as to preserve harmonious coexistence, solidarity, mutual respect, and the common good.

Such an equilibrium in Spain will have positive repercussions in the geographical area to which you belong, and in which you legitimately wish to integrate yourselves more fully. A Spain prosperous and at peace, committed to the promotion of fraternal relations among its peoples, and which does not forget their human, spiritual, and moral identity, can make a valuable contribution to a future of justice and peace in Europe and in the family of nations.

NOVEMBER 2

· · ·

From the address delivered by Pope John Paul II at the Royal Palace, Madrid

BELOW: *The Pope at an evening vigil in Zaragoza.*

CENTRAL AMERICA

March 2 — 9, 1983

A mission of religious nature brings me to Nicaragua; I come as a messenger of peace, as a sustainer of hope, as a servant of faith, to strengthen the faithful in their fidelity to Christ and to his Church; to encourage them with a word of love which may fill souls with sentiments of brotherhood and of reconciliation.

I also come to launch an invitation to peace toward those who, inside or outside this geographical area—wherever they may be—promote in one way or another ideological, economic, or military tensions which impede the free development of these peoples who love peace, brotherhood, and true human, spiritual, social, civil, or democratic progress.

MARCH 4

·   ·   ·

From the discourse delivered at Managua Airport

I do not come with technical or material solutions, which are not within the Church's competence. I bring with me the feeling of nearness, the sympathy, the voice of this Church which supports the just and noble cause of your dignity as men and as children of God.

I know of the conditions of your precarious existence: for many of you, miserable conditions which are frequently less than the fundamental needs of human life.

I know that economic and social development have been unequal in Central America and in this country; I know that the peasant population has often been abandoned to an ignoble level of life and that not a few times it has been harshly treated and exploited.

MARCH 5

·   ·   ·

From John Paul II's address to farm workers, Panama

OPPOSITE: *Walking on a bed of roses in Costa Rica.*

OVERLEAF: *The Pope entertained by native dancers of Panama.*

I know that you are conscious of the inferiority of your social conditions and that you are impatient to obtain a more just distribution of economic goods and a better recognition of the importance and the place due to you in a new and more participating society.

In the search for greater justice and the elevation of your position, you cannot let yourselves be carried away by the temptation to violence, armed guerrilla warfare, or selfish class struggle, because this is not the path of Jesus Christ or of the Church, or of your Christian faith.

A welcoming crowd in Honduras.

Many times, even recently, this nation has been the scene of calamities which have sown death and destruction in many families. And today it continues to suffer the scourge of fratricidal struggles which cause so much pain.

In the name of all the innocent victims, I would like to ask that all forces and all goodwill be mobilized to achieve a peaceful social co-existence, the fruit of justice and of a great reconciliation of souls.

The Church offers you the salvific message of Christ in an attitude of profound respect and love. She is well aware that when she proclaims the Gospel she must be embodied in the peoples who accept the faith and she must assume their cultures.

Your native cultures are the wealth of the peoples, effective ways for transmitting the faith, representations of your relation with God, with men, and with the world. They therefore deserve the greatest respect, esteem, sympathy, and support on the part of all mankind.

These cultures, in fact, have left remarkable monuments—such as those of the Maya, Aztecs, Incas, and many others—which we still contemplate today with wonder.

The work of evangelization does not destroy your values, but is embodied in them, consolidates them, and strengthens them. It gives growth to the seed sown by the Word of God, who before he became flesh in order to save all things and to sum them up in himself, was in the world already as 'the true light that enlightens every man' [Jn 1:9].

But the Church not only respects and evangelizes peoples and cultures. She has always defended the authentic cultural values of every ethnic group.

Also at this time the Church knows, beloved sons and daughters, the social discrimination which you suffer, the injustices that you bear, the serious difficulties you have in defending your lands and your rights, the frequent lack of respect for your customs and traditions.

For this reason, in carrying out her task of evangelization, the Church wants to stay close to you and to raise her voice of condemnation when your dignity as human beings and children of God is violated; she wishes to accompany you peacefully as the Gospel de-

Praying for peace in El Salvador.

mands, but with resolve and energy, in achieving the recognition and the promotion of your dignity and your rights as persons.

For this reason, in this place and in a solemn way, in the name of the Church I ask the government authorities for legislation which effectively protects you from abuses and offers you the surroundings and adequate means for your normal development.

I ask with insistence that the free practice of your Christian faith not be impeded; that no one ever again claim to confuse evangelization with subversion, and that ministers of worship may carry out their mission with safety and without obstacles.

And do not let yourselves be manipulated by ideologies which incite you to violence and death. . . .

I ask that your reservations be respected, and above all that the sacred character of your lives be safeguarded; that no one, for whatever reason, disparage your existence inasmuch as God forbids us to kill and orders us to love one another as brothers.

OPPOSITE: *John Paul II at the cathedral in Managua.*

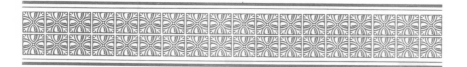

POLAND

June 16 — 23, 1983

I come to my homeland.

The first word, spoken in silence and on bended knee, has been a kiss for this soil, for my native soil.

The kiss placed on the soil of Poland has a particular meaning for me. It is like a kiss placed on the hands of a mother, for the homeland is our earthly mother.

Poland is a special mother. Her history has not been easy, especially over the course of these last centuries. She is a mother who has suffered much and who ever suffers anew. Therefore she also has a right to a special love.

I come to Jasna Gora.

One goes to Jasna Gora on pilgrimage. And so all these days that I will be enabled to spend in my native land will be a pilgrimage.

At the hour of the call of Jasna Gora I stand, O Mother, before your beloved image to greet you.

I salute you as a pilgrim who has come from the See of Saint Peter in Rome, and also as a son of this land, in the midst of which, for six hundred years, you have been present in your image of Jasna Gora.

I am happy that it is given to me today to salute Our Lady of Jasna Gora, first by meditating, and then by singing the call of Jasna Gora together with the Polish youth.

As we say these words—"Mary, Queen of Poland, I am near you, I remember you, I watch"—we do not only bear witness to the spir-

The Pope praying at a tomb in Warsaw Cathedral.

itual presence of the Mother of God among the generations living on Polish soil.

If we say the words of the call of Jasna Gora, we do this not only in order to have recourse to this redemptive and maternal love, but also to respond to this love.

The words "I am near you, I remember you, I watch" are, in fact, at the same time a confession of love, with which we desire to correspond to the love with which we have been eternally loved.

What does it mean "I watch"?

It means that I make an effort to be a person with a conscience. I do not stifle this conscience and I do not deform it; I call good and evil by name, and I do not blur them; I develop in myself what is good, and I seek to correct what is evil, by overcoming it in myself. This is a fundamental problem which can never be minimized or put on a

Paying homage at the memorial to Jewish fighters in the Warsaw ghetto uprising.

The Pope listens to a welcoming address by General Jaruzelski.

secondary level. No! It is everywhere and always a matter of the first importance. Its importance is all the greater in proportion to the increase of circumstances which seem to favor our tolerance of evil and the fact that we easily excuse ourselves from this, especially if adults do so.

My dear friends! It is up to you to put up a firm barrier against immorality, a barrier, I say, to those social vices which I will not call by name but which you yourselves are perfectly aware of. You must demand this of yourselves, even if others do not demand it of you. Historical experiences tell us how much the immorality of certain periods cost the whole nation. Today when we are fighting for the future form of our social life, remember that this form depends on what people will be like. Therefore, watch!

Mother of Jasna Gora, you who have been given to us by Providence for the defenses of the Polish nation, accept this evening this call of the Polish youth together with the Polish Pope, and help us to persevere in hope!

Amen.

LOURDES

August 14 — 15, 1983

Blessed be God! Yes, blessed be God the Father, the Son, and the Holy Spirit, for having prepared here, for Bigorre and the Pyrenees, for France and for the entire Church, such a place of prayers, of crowds and believers, of reconciliation! Blessed be God for having made to gush forth here, one hundred and twenty-five years ago, at the same time as the small spring of Massabielle, a living spring where faith is renewed, 'where bodies and souls are healed, where the meaning of the Church is strengthened! Blessed be God for having done this, once again, through the Virgin Mary who draws the crowds here, just as she attracted Bernadette, to lead them to Christ! Blessed be Our Lady who obtains so many graces for us and who has allowed me, after the attempt on my life from which I was spared, finally to come here to draw from this spring myself and to assemble the faithful here according to the mission of universal Shepherd given to the Apostle Peter.

With you all, I have become a pilgrim. On this earth, in a way, we are always pilgrims and travelers, as Saint Peter put it [1 Pt 2:11].

What message, what Good News, can I give you this evening to guide all our actions?

Simply this: *The Virgin without sin brings help to sinners.*

Quite frankly, our world needs to be converted. It has been this way in every age. In the middle of the nineteenth century, this need manifested itself in a particular way with the unbelief of certain scientific circles, of certain philosophies, and even in daily life. Today, even the sense of sin has partly disappeared, because the meaning of God is being lost. Some have thought of evolving a humanism without God, and the faith might easily be seen as something peculiar to a few, without its necessary role for the salvation of all. Consciences have

AUGUST 14

· · ·

*From the discourse of Pope John Paul II
at Lourdes*

Praying to Our Lady of Lourdes.

become dulled, as on the occasion of the first sin, no longer able to distinguish between good and evil. Many no longer know what sin is, or do not want to know, as if this knowledge would destroy their freedom.

The Virgin without sin reminds us here of this basic need. She tells us, as she told Bernadette: Pray for sinners, come wash yourselves, purify yourselves, draw forth new life. "Reform your lives and believe in the Gospel" [Mk 1:15]. She gives a new meaning to these first words of Jesus in the Gospel.

ABOVE: *Drinking the healing waters of Lourdes.*

RIGHT: *Greeting pilgrims.*

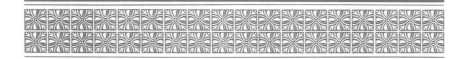

AUSTRIA

September 10 — 13, 1983

These "Europe Vespers" on the occasion of the Austrian *Katholiken-tag* make us look beyond all natural, national, and arbitrary borders to all of Europe, to all the peoples sharing the history of this continent, from the Atlantic to the Urals, from the North Sea to the Mediterranean.

Austria—situated at the very center of Europe—has had a decisive role to play in the fate of Europe and in shaping its history. It demonstrates in an exemplary way how many different peoples can live together, in a small territory, with tensions but creatively, and create unity from diversity. In the small country that Austria is today we find traits of Celts and Romans, of Germanic and Slavic tribes, deeply ingrained and still very much alive in the people of today. In this sense Austria is a mirror of, and a model for, Europe.

Nobody can be oblivious of the fact—a fact which deeply affects us all—that the common history of Europe is marked not only by glorious achievements but also by dark and terrifying events that are incompatible with the spirit of humanity and the Gospel of Jesus Christ. Time and again, nations and factions full of hatred have waged cruel wars against one another. Time and again, people have been deprived of their homes; they have been driven into exile or forced to flee from misery, discrimination, and persecution. Millions of people have been killed, on grounds of their race, their nationality, their convictions, or simply because they were deemed undesirable. It is a depressing thought that devout Christians were among those who oppressed and persecuted their fellow human beings.

While we may justifiably glory in Our Lord Jesus Christ and his message, we have, on the other hand, to confess—and ask forgiveness for the fact—that we Christians have burdened ourselves with

SEPTEMBER 10

· · ·

From the address by the Pope during the celebration of "Europe Vespers" in Vienna

The Pope addressing a Viennese crowd under a statue of Joseph II.

great guilt in thoughts, words, and deeds, and in not standing up against injustice.

However, the history of Europe is marked by discord not only in the sphere of states and politics. Schisms have divided also the one Church of Jesus Christ. In conjunction with political interests and social problems, these have resulted in bitter fighting, in the oppression and expulsion of dissenters, in repression and intolerance. As heirs to our forebears, we also place this guilt-ridden Europe under the Cross. For in the Cross is our hope.

Above all, however, we understand that the language of arms is not the language of Jesus Christ, or of his Mother, who—then as now—was invoked as the "Help of Christians." Armed combat is, at best, an inevitable ill in which even Christians may be tragically and inexorably involved. But here, too, we are under the Christian obligation to love our enemies, to be merciful. He who died on the Cross for his persecutors turns every one of my enemies into a brother of mine, a brother who is worthy of my love even as I defend myself against his onslaught.

A musical interlude in the Austrian Alps.

The Creator has given man the gift of freedom. Thanks to this freedom he can shape and organize the world, create the wonderful products of the human mind with which this country and the world abound: science and the arts, business and technology, our entire civilization. Freedom makes man capable of that unique form of human love which is not merely a consequence of natural attraction but of a free decision of the heart. Freedom makes him capable of the most sublime expression of human dignity: the love and worship of God.

But freedom has its price. All those who are free ought to ask themselves: Have we preserved our dignity in freedom? Freedom does not mean license. Man must not do all he can do or that he wishes to do. There is no freedom without bounds. Man is responsible for himself, for his fellow human beings, for the world. He is responsible to God. Any society that plays down responsibility, law, and conscience will undermine the very foundations of human life. Devoid of a sense of responsibility, man will squander himself in reckless living and, like the prodigal son, suffer the indignities of bondage and lose his home and his freedom. Unrestrained selfishness will make him misuse his fellow man or insatiably strive for material wealth.

Is not all of the history of mankind also a history of the misuse of freedom? Are not many of us following in the steps of the prodigal son? In the end, their lives will be wasted, their love betrayed, their misery self-inflicted, and they will face fear and despair.

*From the homily by Pope John Paul II
delivered at Donaupark, Vienna*

*Raising the Cross at Vienna's Imperial
Palace.*

ASIA

May 2 — 12, 1984

Yours is a beautiful land that, through trials and tempests of a venerable history, has known how to emerge ever new, full of life and youth. Yours is a proud and sturdy people which, in meeting great cultures and neighboring powers, has remained true to its personal identity, bearing splendid fruits in art, religion, and human living. Your ancestors embraced such overwhelming spiritual worlds as Confucianism and Buddhism, yet made them truly their own, enhanced them, lived them, and even transmitted them to others. . . .

So also today the marvelous flowering of the Christian faith in Korea promises to bring spiritual enrichment both to yourselves and to others. The Bicentennial of the Catholic Church in your country gives

MAY 3

·   ·   ·

From the Pope's reply to the welcoming address by the President of Korea at Seoul

OPPOSITE: *His Holiness celebrating Mass.*

BELOW: *The Pope at an ordination of seminarians.*

me the occasion to proclaim that faith in Jesus Christ can indeed bring that enrichment to the culture, wisdom, and dignity of the Korean people.

I speak of the plight of the thousands and thousands of refugees currently living in this country. My deep concern for their welfare and future impels me to mention the subject in this assembly and to speak out on their behalf.

The poverty of these victims of political unrest and civil strife is so extreme on virtually all levels of human existence that it is difficult for the outsider to fathom it. Not only have they lost their material possessions and the work which once enabled them to earn a living for their families and prepare a secure future for their children, but their

MAY 11

· · ·

From the address to the diplomatic corps in Thailand, Bangkok

The Pope giving a gift to Buddhist priests in Bangkok.

Shaking hands with a tribal chief in Samoa.

families themselves have been uprooted and scattered—husbands and wives separated, children separated from their parents. In their native lands they have left behind the tombs of their ancestors, and thus, in a very real way, they have left behind a part of themselves, thereby becoming still poorer.

Many of the refugees have endured great dangers in their flight by sea or land. All too many were given up for lost, or died en route, often the victims of shameless exploitation. Arriving here completely destitute, they have found themselves in a state of total dependence on others to feed them, clothe them, shelter them, and make every decision for their future.

History will record the sense of hospitality, the respect for life, and the deeply rooted generosity shown by the people of Thailand. These national traits have enabled the Thai authorities to overcome many obstacles and thus provide a measure of hope for so many people living on the verge of despair.

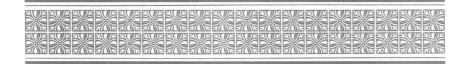

SWITZERLAND

June 12 — 17, 1984

Modern civilization, characterized by the surprisingly rapid development of science and its applications, is going through a deep crisis. But it would be insufficient to content oneself with a diagnosis that is denunciatory, pessimistic, or nostalgic for a dead past. It is most important to find again and to assert the principles of all authentic culture, which principles will enable mankind to work in a truly constructive way. Our period and the periods that preceded it too easily believed that scientific and technological conquests would be the equivalent, or at least the guarantee, of human progress, which progress would bring about freedom and happiness. In our own days, many scholars as well as an increasing number of our contemporaries are realizing that the rash transformation of the world risks jeopardizing in a grave way the complex and delicate equilibrium that exists in nature. They feel deep anxiety at the technical achievements that are liable to become terrifying instruments of destruction and death, as also at other recent discoveries, heavy with menaces of the manipulation and enslavement of man. This is why some are tempted to throw discredit on the great modern venture of science as such. Moreover, an ever-increasing number of scientists are becoming aware of their human responsibility and are convinced that there cannot be science without conscience. This fundamental thought is a positive and encouraging gain of our own time, which is better able to measure the limits of scientism, which one should take good care not to identify with science itself.

JUNE 13

From the address by the Pope at the
University of Freiburg

OVERLEAF: *Greeting children of Lucerne.*

CANADA

September 4 — 20, 1984

In today's Gospel, Christ stands before us as our Judge. He has a special right to make this judgment; indeed he became one of us, our Brother. This brotherhood with the human race—and at the same time his brotherhood with every single person—has led him to the Cross and the Resurrection.

Thus he judges in the name of his solidarity with each person and likewise in the name of our solidarity with him, who is our Brother and Redeemer and whom we discover in every human being: "I was hungry . . . I was thirsty . . . I was a stranger . . . naked . . . sick . . . in prison . . ." [Mt 25:35–36].

And those called to judgment—on his right hand and on his left—will ask: When and where? When and where have we seen you like this? When and where have we done what you said? Or: When and where have we not done it?

The answer: "Truly, I say to you, as you did it to one of the least of these my brethren, you did it to me" [Mt 25:45]. And, on the contrary: "As you did it not to one of the least of these, you did it not to me" [Mt 25:45].

"To one of the least of these my brethren"—thus to man, to an individual human being in need.

Yet the Second Vatican Council, following the whole of tradition, warns us not to stop at an individualistic interpretation of Christian ethics, since Christian ethics also has its social dimension. The human person lives in a community, in society. And with the community he shares hunger and thirst and sickness and malnutrition and misery and all the deficiencies that result therefrom. In his or her own

SEPTEMBER 17

· · ·

From the homily delivered by Pope John Paul II at Edmonton, Alberta

ABOVE: *The Pope talks with Indian children.*

In the light of Christ's words, this poor South will judge the rich North. And the poor people and poor nations . . . will judge those people who take these goods away from them.

Gymnasts paying homage in Montreal.

person the human being is meant to experience the needs of others.

So it is that Christ the Judge speaks of "one of the least of the brethren," and at the same time he is speaking of each and of all.

Yes. He is speaking of the whole universal dimension of injustice and evil. He is speaking of what today we are accustomed to call the North-South contrast. Hence not only East-West, but also North-South: the increasingly wealthier North, and the increasingly poorer South.

Yes, the South—becoming always poorer; and the North—becoming always richer. Richer, too, in the resources of weapons with which the superpowers and blocs can mutually threaten each other. And they threaten each other—such an argument also exists—in order not to destroy each other.

This is a separate dimension—and according to the opinion of many it is the dimension in the forefront—of the deadly threat which hangs over the modern world and which deserves separate attention.

Nevertheless, in the light of Christ's words, this poor South will judge the rich North. And the poor people and poor nations—poor in different ways, not only lacking food, but also deprived of freedom and other human rights—will judge those people who take these goods away from them, amassing to themselves the imperialistic monopoly of economic and political supremacy at the expense of others. . . .

May the God of peace be with us! This cry brings with it the whole drama of our age, the whole threat. The nuclear threat? Certainly! But even more, the whole threat of injustice, the threat coming from the rigid structures of those systems which man is not able to pass through—those systems which do not open themselves so as to permit themselves to go out toward man, to go out toward the development of peoples, to go out toward justice, with all its requirements, and toward peace.

Is the global balance not perhaps ever increasing—the global balance of what we "have not done for one of the least of the brethren"? For millions of the least of the brethren? For billions?

This must also be said here, in Canada, which is as vast as a continent. And at the same time here, from this very place, it must likewise be said to all people of goodwill, and to all groups, communities, organizations, institutions, nations, and governments, that everything we "have done" and what we will still do, what we will plan and will do with ever greater energy and determination—all of this really matters.

Blessing a fountain.

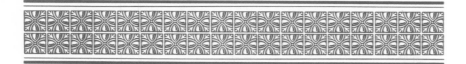

THE DOMINICAN REPUBLIC AND PUERTO RICO

October 10 — 12, 1984

In its human aspect, the arrival of the discoverers at Guanahani meant a fantastic widening of mankind's frontiers, the mutual discovery of two worlds, the appearance of the entire inhabited world before the eyes of man, the beginning of universal history in its process of interaction, with all its benefits and contradictions, its lights and shadows.

In its evangelizing aspect, it marked an unprecedented missionary unfolding which, starting from the Iberian Peninsula, would soon give a new configuration to the ecclesial map.

A certain "black legend" which marked not a few historiographical studies for some time concentrated its attention primarily on aspects of violence and exploitation which occurred in civil society during the period which followed discovery. Political, ideological, and even religious prejudices have also negatively presented the history of the Church on this continent.

She does not wish to ignore the interdependence that existed between the cross and the sword in the phases of the first missionary penetration. But neither does she wish to forget that the spread of Iberian Christianity brought to the new peoples the gift inherent in the origins and development of Europe—the Christian faith—with its charge of humanity and its capacity for salvation, dignity and fraternity, justice and love, for the New World.

But in spite of the excessive nearness or confusion between the lay and religious spheres common to that era, there was no absorption or submission, and the voice of the Church was raised against sin from the first moment.

OCTOBER 12

· · ·

From the message delivered by Pope John Paul II in Santo Domingo, Dominican Republic

Resist the seduction of ideologies which try to substitute the idols of power and violence, riches and pleasure for the Christian view.

John Paul II prepares to give Communion in Santo Domingo.

In the heart of a society inclined to see the material benefits that it could gain by slavery and by the exploitation of the Indians, there arose the clear protest of the critical conscience of the Gospel, which denounced the non-observance of the demands of human dignity and brotherhood, which have their foundation in creation and the divine filiation of all persons.

So the Church, faced with the sin of man, including her own children, tried to bring at that time, as in other eras, the grace of conversion, hope of salvation, solidarity with the defenseless, and an effort for integral liberation.

The impelling cry for a justice that it too long awaited is raised by a society that seeks its due dignity.

Corruption in public life, armed conflicts, huge expenditures to procure death and not progress, the lack of ethical sentiment in so many fields, all cause weariness and destroy dreams of a better future.

To all of this are added the rivalries among nations, incorrect behavior in international relations and in commercial interchanges, which create new imbalances. And now there is the serious problem of the foreign debt of the Third World countries, especially of Latin America.

This phenomenon can create conditions of social paralysis of in-definite duration and can condemn entire nations to a permanent debt, with grave repercussions, which can cause permanent under-development.

Resist the temptation of those who want to forget your undeniable Christian vocation and the values that shape it, in order to seek so-cial models that prescind from it or contradict it.

Resist the temptation of whatever can weaken communion in the Church as a sacrament of unity and salvation—whether it be from those who make an ideology of the faith or claim to build a "popular Church" which is not that of Christ, or whether it be from those who promote the spread of religious sects which have little to do with the true contents of the faith.

Resist the anti-Christian temptation of those who do not believe in dialogue and reconciliation and resort to violence, and who substi-tute the power of arms or ideological oppression for political solu-tions.

Resist the seduction of ideologies which try to substitute the idols of power and violence, riches and pleasure for the Christian view.

Resist the corruption of public life and of the merchants of drugs and pornography, which are eroding the moral fiber, the resistance, and the hope of peoples.

Resist the action of the agents of neo-Malthusianism who want to impose a new colonialism on the Latin American peoples, weakening their life force with contraceptive practices, sterilization, and the lib-eralization of abortion, and disintegrating the unity, the stability, and the fertility of the family.

Resist the egoism of the "satisfied" who cling to the privileges of an opulent minority, while vast sectors of the people endure difficult and even dramatic living conditions in situations of misery, emar-gination, and oppression.

Resist the interference of foreign powers, who follow their own economic interests, whether bloc or ideological, and reduce peoples to tactical maneuvers fields in the service of their own strategies.

The coming fifth centenary of the discovery and the first evangeli-zation calls us then to a new evangelization of Latin America, which will develop more vigorously, as it did in its beginnings, a potential for sanctity, a great missionary thrust, a vast creativity in catechesis, a fruitful manifestation of collegiality and communion, and an evan-gelical battle for the dignity of man, in order to generate a great fu-ture of hope in the bosom of Latin America.

SOUTH AMERICA

January 26 — February 6, 1985

I did not wish to omit a visit to Ayacucho during my apostolic journey in Peru. In it I wish to draw near to the suffering of the inhabitants of this region, to give you a word of encouragement and contribute to the longed-for reconciliation of spirits.

In these regions—as, alas, in others of this beloved country—is heard the anguished cry of its peoples who plead for peace. I know that there is much suffering due to the spiral of violence that has its center among you. I share from the depth of my heart the wounds you suffer. May the suffering that afflicts your families end quickly, and in the meantime may you know how to endure it with an evangelical spirit, which does not mean cowardice but rather courage to react with dignity, resorting to legitimate means of protecting society, and not to violence which engenders more violence.

Your difficult challenge is to combat this violence with the arms of

FEBRUARY 3

· · ·

From the Pope's address in Ayacucho, Peru

OPPOSITE: *The Pope greets the natives of Latacunga.*

ABOVE: *The Pope at a Mass with Virgin and Child in Lima.*

peace and to convince those who have fallen into the temptation of hatred that only love is effective. . . .

It is necessary that convinced Christians—experts in the various fields of knowledge and at the same time acquainted through their own experience with the political, economic, and social sectors—reflect in depth on the problems of contemporary society, in order to illuminate them by the light of the Gospel.

The international community, for its part, and the institutions operating in the field of cooperation among nations, should apply just measures in relations, above all in economic relations with developing countries. They should put aside all discriminatory action in commercial exchanges, above all in the market of raw materials. In offering the necessary financial aid they must seek, by joint agreement, conditions that allow those peoples to rise out of a situation of poverty and underdevelopment, refraining from imposing financial conditions which, in the long run, instead of helping these peoples to improve their situation, make it even worse, and can even lead them to desperate circumstances which bring conflicts whose magnitude it is impossible to calculate.

AFRICA

August 8 — 19, 1985

God said to Adam and Eve: "Be fruitful and multiply, and fill the earth and subdue it; and have dominion over the fish of the sea and over the birds of the air and over every living thing that moves upon the earth" [Gen 1:28].

It is a requirement of our human dignity, and therefore a serious responsibility, to exercise dominion over creation in such a way that it truly serves the human family. Exploitation of the riches of nature must take place according to the criteria that take into account not only immediate needs, but also the needs of future generations. In this way the stewardship over nature, entrusted by God to man, will not be guided by shortsightedness or selfish pursuits; rather, it will take into account the fact that all created goods are directed to the good of all humanity. The use of natural resources must aim at serving the integral development of present and future generations. Progress in the field of ecology, and growing awareness of the need to protect and conserve certain nonrenewable natural resources, are in keeping with the demands of true stewardship. God is glorified when creation serves the integral development of the whole human family.

With the rapid acceleration of science and technology in recent decades, the environment has been subjected to far greater changes than ever before. As a result, we are offered many new opportunities for development and human progress; we are now able to transform our surroundings greatly, even dramatically, for the enhancement of the quality of life. On the other hand, this new ability, unless it is used with wisdom and vision, can cause tremendous and even irreparable harm in the ecological and social spheres. The capacity for improving the environment and the capacity for destroying it increase enormously each year.

AUGUST 18

· · ·

From the Pope's address to United Nations officials in Nairobi, Kenya

John Paul II with the King of Morocco at the palace in Casablanca.

With native dignitaries of Cameroon.

The ultimate determining factor is the human person. It is not science and technology, or the increasing means of economic and material development, but the human person and especially groups of persons—communities and nations—freely choosing to face the problems together, who will, under God, determine the future. That is why whatever impedes human freedom or dishonors it, such as the evil of apartheid and all forms of prejudice and discrimination, is an affront to man's vocation to shape his own destiny. Eventually it will have repercussions in all areas requiring human freedom and as such can become a major stumbling block to the improvement of the environment and all of society.

Normally, the young look toward the future, they long for a more just and more human world. God made young people thus, precisely that they might help to transform the world in accordance with his plan of life. But to them, too, the situation often appears to have its shadows.

In this world there are frontiers and divisions between men, as also misunderstandings between the generations; there are, likewise, racism, wars, and injustices, and also hunger, waste, and unemployment. These are the dramatic evils which touch us all, more particularly the young of the entire world. Some are in danger of discouragement, others of capitulation, others of willing to change everything by violence or by extreme solutions. Wisdom teaches us that self-discipline and love are then the only means to the desired renewal.

God does not will that people should remain passive. This world, which is about to come, depends on the young people of all the countries of the world. Our world is divided, and even shattered; it experiences multiple conflicts and grave injustices. There is no real North-South solidarity; there is not enough mutual assistance between the nations of the South. There are in the world cultures and races which are not respected.

Clasping hands with African youths in Kinshasa.

Why is all this? It is because people do not accept their differences; they do not know each other sufficiently. They reject those who have not the same civilization. They refuse to help each other. They are unable to free themselves from egoism and from self-conceit.

But God created all men equal in dignity, though different with regard to gifts and to talents. Mankind is a whole where each one has his part to play; the worth of the various peoples and of the diverse cultures must be recognized. The world is, as it were, a living organism; each culture has something to receive from the others, and has something to give to them.

I am happy to meet you here in Morocco. Morocco has a tradition of openness. Your scholars have traveled, and you have welcomed scholars from other countries. Morocco has been a meeting place of civilizations: it has permitted exchanges with the East, with Spain, and with Africa. Morocco has a tradition of tolerance. In this Muslim country there have always been Jews and nearly always Christians; that tradition has been carried out in respect, in a positive manner. You have been, and you remain, a hospitable country. You, young Moroccans, are then prepared to become citizens of tomorrow's world, of this fraternal world to which, with the young people of all the world, you aspire.

ABOVE: *Accepting refreshment in Togo.*

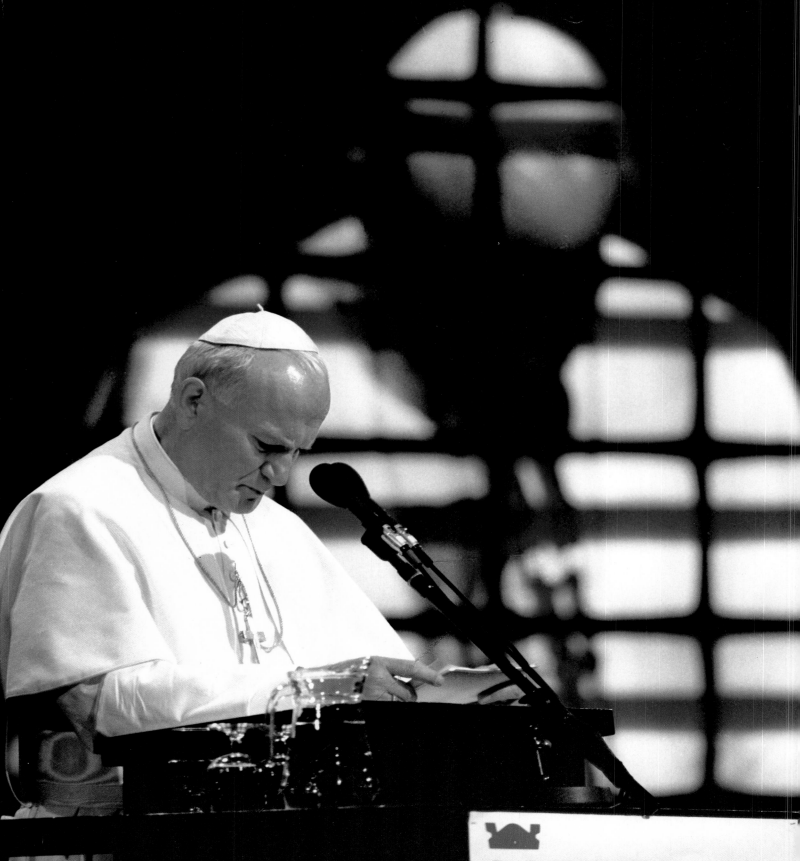

BELGIUM, THE NETHERLANDS, AND LUXEMBOURG

May 5 — 21, 1985

To say "Our Father . . . give us this day our daily bread" is to ask that every man, here and throughout the world, might be able to satisfy his hunger and have access to that which allows him to live with dignity; and it is also to prepare oneself to work toward this end, in order to bring about better production, distribution, and utilization of created goods. It is also to strive to allow every person to find employment so that he can worthily earn a living. It is to question ourselves regarding the meaning that we give to earning, sharing, study, free time, and creativity.

To say "Our Father . . . forgive us our sins" is to ask God for our reconciliation with him, which we cannot obtain by ourselves; it is also to employ all our energy in order to understand others, to pardon, to be architects of peace, to exclude no one. To say "Our Father . . . lead us not into temptation" is to ask God for the lucidity and the strength to avoid the deceptions by means of which our society exploits the weak, by means of which the evil one exploits our weaknesses and our passions: the promise of immediate and easy enjoyment, unbridled sexuality, drugs of every sort, artificial paradises, costly fads, the uproar which degrades man, dealers in illusions and evasion, all the modern idols which maintain our selfishness in all its forms.

To say "Our Father . . . deliver us from evil" is to struggle within and around ourselves against that which aims at destroying the faith: indifference, systematic doubt, skepticism, as if happiness and the grandeur of man consisted in his liberating himself from God. It is to struggle against despair and disgust with life, as though life no longer

MAY 18

· · ·

From the Pope's address to young people at Brussels, Belgium

An address in Utrecht.

To say "Our Father . . . deliver us from evil" is to struggle within and around ourselves against that which aims at destroying the faith: indifference, systematic doubt, skepticism.

ABOVE: *At an industrial site in Luxembourg.*

LEFT: *A special gift from the bakers of Mechelen.*

had meaning. It is to struggle against deviations from love, the seduction of violence and hate, justified as means for efficaciously changing the world without changing hearts. It is to struggle, in short, against falsehood and the father of lies.

As the rain causes the seed to sprout, may your prayer, starting tomorrow, keep these words and make them resound within you! As the sower awaits the growth of his crops with patience, may your confidence as sons of God allow the Spirit to guide your maturation in the days ahead.

As the farmer busily goes to work at harvest time, may you dispose your intelligence and your hearts to be present and active wherever men and women lift up their heads and unite to create a renewed world, according to the heart of God.

BELOW: *Homage to the victims of World War I at Ypres.*

INDIA

February 1 — 10, 1986

It is entirely fitting that this pilgrimage should begin here, at Raj Ghat, dedicated to the memory of the illustrious Mahatma Gandhi, the Father of the Nation and apostle of nonviolence.

The figure of Mahatma Gandhi and the meaning of his life's work have penetrated the consciousness of humanity. In his famous words, Pandit Jawaharlal Nehru has expressed the conviction of the whole world: "The light that shone in this country was no ordinary light."

Two days ago marked the thirty-eighth anniversary of his death. He who lived by nonviolence appeared to be defeated by violence. For a brief moment, the light seemed to have gone out. Yet his teachings and the example of his life lives on in the minds and hearts of millions of men and women. And so it was said: "The light has gone out of our lives and there is darkness everywhere and I do not quite know what to tell you and how to say it. . . . The light has gone out, I said, and yet I was wrong. For the light that shone in this country was no ordinary light. The light that has illumined this country for these many years will illumine this country for many more years."

Yes, the light is still shining, and the heritage of Mahatma Gandhi speaks to us still. And today, as a pilgrim of peace I have come here to pay homage to Mahatma Gandhi, hero of humanity.

From this place, which is forever bound to the memory of this extraordinary man, I wish to express to the people of India and of the world my profound conviction that the peace and justice of which contemporary society has such great need will be achieved only along the path that was at the core of his teaching: the supremacy of the spirit and *Satyagraha*, the "truth-force" which conquers without violence by the dynamism intrinsic to just action.

ABOVE: *Greeting the Dalai Lama.*

OPPOSITE: *The Pilgrim of Peace expresses kinship with Mahatma Gandhi, a man of peace.*

OVERLEAF: *A traditional Indian welcome.*

The power of truth leads us to recognize with Mahatma Gandhi the dignity, equality, and fraternal solidarity of all human beings, and it prompts us to reject every form of discrimination. It shows us once again the need for mutual understanding, acceptance, and collaboration between religious groups in the pluralist society of modern India and throughout the world.

The traditional problems of poverty, hunger, and disease have not yet been eradicated from our world. Indeed, in some ways they are more virulent than ever. In addition, new sources of tension and anxiety have emerged. The existence of immense arsenals of weapons of mass destruction causes a grave and justified uneasiness in our minds. The inequality of development favors some and plunges others into inextricable dependence. In these conditions, peace is fragile and injustice abounds.

From this place, which belongs in a sense to the history of the entire human family, I wish, however, to reaffirm the conviction that with the help of God the construction of a better world, in peace and justice, lies within the reach of human beings.

As man on this earth passes from birth to death, he is aware of being a pilgrim of the Absolute. Here in India this consciousness is very deep. Your ancient sages have expressed the anguished cry of the soul for the Absolute. There is indeed an age-old yearning for the infinite, a constant awareness of the divine presence, and endless manifestations of religious feelings through popular feasts and festivals.

India has so much to offer the world in the task of understanding man and the truth of his existence. And what she offers specifically is a noble spiritual vision of man—man, a pilgrim of the Absolute, traveling toward a goal, seeking the face of God. Did not Mahatma Gandhi put it this way: "What I want to achieve—what I have been striving and pining to achieve . . . is self-realization—to see God face to face. I live and move and have my being in pursuit of this goal."

On the rectitude of this spiritual vision is built the defenses of man in his daily life. With this spiritual vision of man we are equipped to

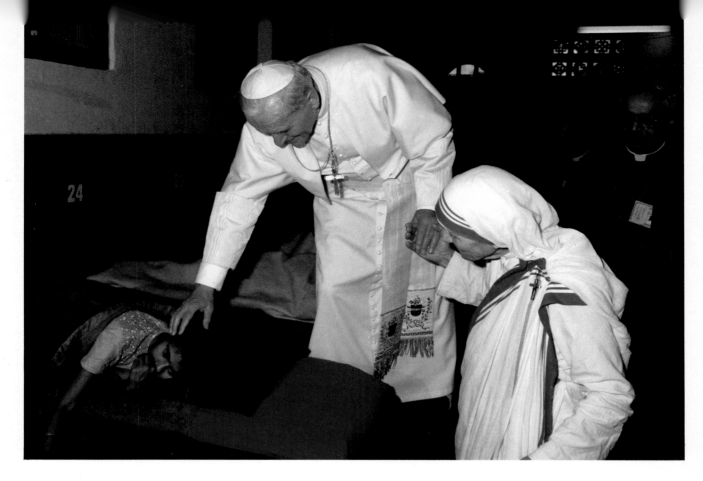

Visiting the sick with Mother Teresa.

face the concrete problems that affect man, torment his soul, and afflict his body.

From this vision comes the incentive to undertake the struggle to remedy and improve man's condition, and to pursue relentlessly his integral human development.

In India, without doubt, this reality offers us a spiritual vision of man. I believe that this spiritual vision is of supreme relevance for the people of India and for their future; it says much about their values, their hopes and aspirations, and their human dignity. I believe that a spiritual vision of man is of immense importance for the whole of humanity. With an emphasis on spiritual values, the world is capable of formulating a new attitude toward itself—new, but based to a great extent on ethical values preserved for centuries, many of them in this ancient land. These include a spirit of fraternal charity and dedicated service, forgiveness, sacrifice and renunciation, remorse and penance for moral failings, and patience and forbearance.

With the passing of time, it becomes evident that it is necessary to return over and over again to the central issue of the world, which is *man*: man as a creature and child of God; man bearing within his heart and soul the image and likeness of God; man destined to fulfill his calling to live forever.